T0194704

21 DAYS
MYTH

21 DAYS
MYTH

HABITS & LEADERSHIP

Jonathan Lopez

21 DAYS MYTH
HABITS & LEADERSHIP

iUniverse books may be ordered through booksellers or by contacting:

iUniverse
1663 Liberty Drive
Bloomington, IN 47403
www.iuniverse.com
1-800-Authors (1-800-288-4677)

ISBN: 978-1-5320-8097-5 (sc)
ISBN: 978-1-5320-8098-2 (e)

Library of Congress Control Number: 2019912611

Print information available on the last page.

iUniverse rev. date: 08/27/2019

Scripture quotations from the Holy Bible, King James Version (Authorized Version). First published in 1611. Quoted from the KJV Classic Reference Bible.

Scripture quotations marked NIV are taken from the Holy Bible, New International Version®. NIV®. Copyright © 1973, 1978, 1984 by International Bible Society. Used by permission of Zondervan. All rights reserved. [Biblica]

Unless otherwise indicated, all scripture quotations are from The Holy Bible, English Standard Version® (ESV®). Copyright ©2001 by Crossway Bibles, a division of Good News Publishers. Used by permission. All rights reserved.

Scripture quotations marked NRSV are taken from the New Revised Standard Version of the Bible, Copyright © 1989, by the Division of Christian Education of the National Council of the Churches of Christ in the United States of America. Used by permission. All rights reserved. WebsiteUndo

INTRODUCTION

In this book, I broke down the idea and myths about the concept of creating a habit in 21 days. What does it takes to become a successful person and improve yourself?

Discipline is the most common trait in a successful person or leader. By presenting you with scientific and medical facts and personal experiences, I opened myself up to you in this book to provide you guidance in your journey to success. By being a part of the military and law enforcement, I have seen some common mistakes of those who have failed in these arenas and how some of those people were able to get back on their feet and become a successful person.

Regardless of your background or history, you should have no excuses because after reading this book, you will become a better asset to your company or agency, a better entrepreneur in your business, and you will have received important tools to better yourself and life of your family.

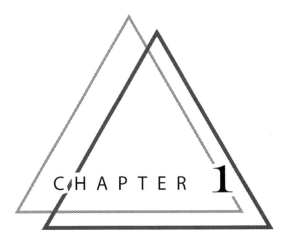

CHAPTER 1

21 DAYS MYTH

"Your net worth to the world is usually determined by what remains after your bad habits are subtracted from your good ones."

- Benjamin Franklin (1706-1790)

How many times you have seen or heard that in order to create or eliminate a habit you need to repeat the same actions or behaviors for at least 21 consecutive days? This concept started with Maxwell Maltz (1889-1975), a plastic surgeon back in the 1950s. He came up with the concept after noticing that his patients were taking about 3 weeks to get used to any form of plastic surgery. The concept became very popular and later in the 1960s, he published the book *Psycho Cybernetics* a motivational inspiration for the public.

To investigate the process of habit formation in everyday life, 96 volunteers chose an eating, drinking or activity behavior to carry out daily in the same context (for example 'after breakfast') for 12 weeks. They completed the self-report habit index (SRHI) each day and recorded whether they carried out the behavior. The majority (82) of participants provided enough data for analysis and increases in automaticity (calculated with a sub-set of SRHI items) were examined over the study period.

Nonlinear regressions fitted an asymptotic curve to everyone's automaticity scores over the 84 days. The model fitted for 62 individuals, of whom 39 showed a good fit. Performing the behavior more consistently was associated with better model fit. The time it took participants to reach 95% of their asymptote of automaticity ranged from 18 to 254 days; indicating considerable variation in how long it takes people to reach their limit of automaticity and highlighting that it can take a very long time. Missing one opportunity to perform the behavior did not materially affect the habit formation process. With repetition of a behavior in a consistent context, automaticity increases following an asymptotic curve which can be modelled at the individual level.

Copyright © 2009 John Wiley & Sons, Ltd. (Lally, 2009)

Now that we understand the concept of the 21-day habit and the origins of it, it will be easier to help yourself become a successful person by developing the discipline of good habits that will follow you everywhere you go, and will affect those around you in a positive manner.

After the study conducted by Phillippa Lally, it was determined that an individual can take anywhere from 18 days up to 254 days to develop a habit. That does, however, depend on the individual's self-control, current mindset, and ability to focus. Typically, most people would like to be successful in life, to stay healthy, and to become a wealthy person, but not everyone is willing to pay the price or to develop the discipline needed to reach their goals.

Frustration is created when individuals have the expectation that changing their lifetime behavior or bad habit will only take 21 days to change. After those 21 days, the people who are not able to create or break said habit become upset and perhaps feel like failures. These individuals may start to feel like they are not capable of changing their life, whether they are trying to get rid of a bad habit or trying to get used to a new one.

Back in 2010. I worked for a financial planning company (commission based) in Puerto Rico and they always used the 21 days concept in every meeting I attended. It was always claimed that we would be successful by repeating the same actions for 21 days. The result was that, on average, 1 in every 10 individuals that joined the commission-based job were able to succeed, and the other 9 were either quitting or keeping a low income while continuing to do it only part-time. In the meantime, the office manager was earning $150,000 dollars a year, and on the small island of Puerto Rico, that is a lot of money. This is another example of how the 21 days concept is overrated and exploited in the wrong way, creating confusion and proving that it is just another myth. Now, you may be asking:

What does it really take to become successful by developing good habits?
How are our brains wired?
How do successful people become successful?

In the next pages, you will find the scientific facts on how we can train ourselves to successfully develop good habits.

A smoker would probably take more than 21 days to quit. Now, some people will use patches, and some will quit "cold turkey" right away. Why?

Some people will work out in the gym every morning, and some are not be able to wake up early and workout.

Some people will make their bed as soon they get up and some would not even worry about it.

Something we can find behind every successful person is discipline, or self-control. That is one of the common traits that we can find in every millionaire (not counting people that win the lottery).

There is a high percentage of people with no discipline that win the lottery and 5 years later they find themselves in the same or worst situation. Again, ask yourself: *Why?*

> Economist Jay L. Zagorsky agrees with the research. He writes for U.S. News and World Report: "Studies found that instead of getting

people out of financial trouble, winning the lottery got people into more trouble, since bankruptcy rates soared for lottery winners three to five years after winning. (Hess, 2017)

This lack of discipline and planning create the worst scenarios. For the most part, most lottery winners complain about the same issues.

i.e.

> Jack Whittaker, who won $315 million in a lottery in West Virginia in 2002, tells Time, "I wish that we had torn the ticket up." Since winning, Whittaker's daughter and granddaughter died due to drug overdoses.
>
> Just eight months after winning, he was robbed of $545,000. "I just don't like Jack Whittaker. I don't like the hard heart I've got," he said. "I don't like what I've become."
>
> McNay says many winners struggle with suicide, depression and divorce. "It's the curse of the lottery because it made their lives worse instead of improving them," he says.
>
> Another major struggle that winners often face is saying "no" to friends and family who hope to join in on the good fortune." (Hess, 2017)

By breaking down the 21 days myth, you will be able to avoid being another victim and set yourself up for success. There is a famous saying that you might have heard before:

*"You can lead a horse to water, but you can't make it drink".
(Common Proverb - Unknown)*

After this breakdown, it's clear that the 21 days concept can be placed under "fiction status," and you can start focusing on what really matters: the changes you need to make and the discipline that you will need to apply to avoid disappointments when you can't achieve your goals or habit during those "21 days". The next chapter will uncover the science behind our minds.

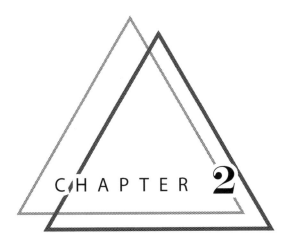

UNCOVER THE SECRETS

"How many people are trapped in their everyday habits:
part numb, part frightened, part indifferent? To have a
better life we must keep choosing how we are living."

- Albert Einstein (1879-1955)

Oxford dictionary define habit as a settled or regular pattern, tendency, or practice, especially one that is hard to give up. Have you ever asked yourself why it's easier to develop or adopt a bad habit rather than a good habit? Our brains are wired to go through the path of least resistance. In other words, the concept of "fight or flight" is in our human nature. It's important to mention that habits are not only actions, but also thoughts. Our brain develops a pattern after repeated actions or thoughts. I've used this in the military and in law enforcement for training. When we face a stressful situation, our fine motor skills are limited and only the gross motor skills are the ones capable to perform a task. For example, if you're an officer, you will receive several trainings a year on how to respond to shootings, etc. When the real-life situation hits you, your brain will fall back to your second nature and how you train; you will always fall back to your training. In the military, we used the concept "train as we fight," because history and real-life scenarios shows that under a stressful situation, your body will naturally do what is used to do. It's also called "second nature."

Fine v. Gross motor skills

Fine motor skill (or dexterity) is the coordination of small muscles, in movements usually involving the synchronization of hands and fingers with the eyes. The complex levels of manual dexterity that humans exhibit can be attributed to and demonstrated in tasks controlled by the nervous system. Fine motor skills aid in the growth of intelligence and develop continuously throughout the stages of human development." (Wikipedia, n.d.)

Gross motor (physical) skills are those which require whole body movement, and which involve the large (core stabilizing) muscles of the body to perform everyday functions, such as standing, walking, running, and sitting upright. It also includes eye-hand coordination skills such as ball skills (throwing, catching, kicking). (Kid Sense, n.d.)

We need to become positive thinkers, people who talk positively to ourselves and who start looking at things in life from a positive perspective, the kind of people that see the cup half-full and not half-empty. By doing this, you are rewiring your brain, training yourself to become a positive thinker and, like I mentioned before, during the hard times or stressful situations, your body and brain will fall back to your training, your newfound positive second nature. Now, we can establish that developing habits can be translated to doing things in autopilot mode. Making your bed, tying your shoes, and brushing your teeth are some of the things most of us automatically do.

The good news is that our brain is an amazing computer and can register and learn new behaviors. You are in control; a bad situation cannot be the deterrent of your success, and it cannot be the wall. It's up to you if you want to bounce back stronger than ever with a positive mindset.

Science of Change

"In order to create,
equilibrium must be broken."
— **Daniel Parris**

Cells are constantly receiving information and constantly replicating themselves. If we have been constantly feeding them cortisol, anxiety, etc. they have replicated more receptors that emotion. When you do a repeated action, or feel a repeated emotion, it becomes a habit - when you do the habit you have learned, your brain produces serotonin, dopamine and endorphins, which makes it hard not to do it.

In other words, if you worry all the time, and it has become a habit, even though you do not want to do it, your brain automatically takes that path because it is the most familiar and thinks that is the right state to be in.

Same with any bad habit or addiction. When you do it, you produce serotonin and dopamine and endorphins, which make it hard not to do it. Like checking your phone all the time for example.

When stopping a habit or way of thinking, you will go through a bit of transition phase- as in your cells are literally withdrawing because you are not giving them what they are used to.

The great news is when you start doing something new- your brain begins to create new receptor sites and new neural pathways!

However, the feeling of this happening gets people tripped up. When they feel the withdrawal from the cells, they assign a meaning to that feeling of "this is uncomfortable, this is hard" or "this does not feel right, I'll try again another time."

Feeling resistance is the BEST signal that something BIG is happening. You need to assign a positive message to that feeling of resistance and you become unstoppable because you know that in just a short time, your brain will be completely rewired.

> This gives people relief knowing what is happening so they can expect it and know that they are not weak or lack willpower, they are just rewiring their brain, and the feeling of withdrawal is real, but will go away. (Kelly, 2016)

Being in the military helped me to develop a strong core when it comes down to improving myself and helping others to do the same. One tool I use and translate into my personal life is the Operational Order (OPORD). That's part of the troop leading procedures I learned and used most of the time by my commanders to issue an order/mission to a brigade, battalion or unit.

At the highest level, the chain of command receives the vision, then they turn that vision into a plan; that plan becomes the mission that we later execute. Our brain is no different; we need to establish a vision in our mind and subconscious in order to execute a mission. Without a vision, we cannot have a plan; therefore, no mission will be executed.

It's important to understand this concept and start to change our viewpoint as things happen to us. Sometimes we are in control of certain situations, and sometimes we need to adapt and overcome a situation that we did not want or could not control anymore.

You have the power to decide where you're going to be in the next year, in the next 5 years, and in the next 10, but you will need to visualize your goals, write them down, and develop a plan. Don't expect to get there in a day, but make sure you do something. Whether it's something big or small, make sure there is something for you to work on that will bring you closer to that goal and dream. Sometimes we cannot avoid certain situations, but we can certainly control our reactions to each situation.

Establishing a vision is very important; you need to know what you want, then you can start doing everything you can to move you closer to that vision.

Identifying your weakness and strengths is another big step to take during your journey. Listening to the people around you for good quality constructive criticism. Choose wisely; listen to those that always bring something good to the table. If someone is talking about how to improve your credit score, that person should have a great credit score 700+. Keep in mind, though that you cannot listen to everyone's opinion because you will never be able to please everyone.

Credibility is one of the filters you need to apply to analyze the people around you. Use that credibility filter to know which advice you should listen to.

Another helpful thing you can do is make a list of the strengths and weaknesses that you know you have. Then ask people that are close to you (family, good friends, supporters) what they think you should do to improve as a person. Sometimes it's good to know how our whole picture looks from the outside and from others' point of view. In the military, we used the term AAR (After Actions Review). This was conducted after every training or mission. This type of review helps to keep up the good things about ourselves and avoid repeating mistakes in the future. It's not like you are going to hold yourself back because someone doesn't share the same vision as you do, but it's a helpful thing to see yourself how others see you.

How many times someone do you hear someone complaining about a task you love to do?

How many times do you hear someone complaining about something you consider a blessing?

Perspective is always a great thing to keep in mind because it is always good to receive some kind of counseling from a friend, a mentor, or family member to help us see and understand their different points of view.

Make sure you surround yourself with people that are open minded, successful, and an inspiration to others. There's an old saying that goes, "You're a product of who you surround yourself with." Make sure you cover that in your mental checklist. During this process, you will find out that sometimes family become strangers and strangers become family. Keep in mind that you might know how to execute a mission, but if your plan isn't right, you'll fail. On the other hand, you might know how to develop a plan without knowing how to start. These two concepts are meant to be together; work on both of them and make sure you have a mentor with the right experience to guide you.

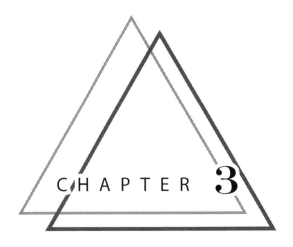

CHAPTER 3

HOW TO BECOME A
SUCCESSFUL LEADER

*"Average leaders raise the bar on themselves;
good leaders raise the bar for others; great
leaders inspire others to raise their own bar."*

- Orrin Woodward

I. Servant Leader V. Followership

In this chapter, you will be able to understand the characteristics of a servant leader, followership, and the differences between the two and the similarities. It's very important to understand that while we all need each other and cannot operate alone, everyone cannot be a leader; in a hierarchy structure, we need a balance between leaders and those in a subordinate role. Understanding this will help you to be successful in everything you do. Apply yourself and visualize your life from a different perspective. A leader will need to be a good follower before he becomes a great leader. Good leaders are followed by the team without hesitation.

The question is, how? It's easy to say, "Go and be a good leader," but you need to be able to put it in practice on a daily basis and teach others to be effective in their careers and duties. In my opinion, the characteristics of a servant leader are as follows: someone that leads from the front and is capable of doing the things that they demand from their subordinates, and someone that helps to develop others to become good leaders by offering mentorship and the tools needed for this. Bad leadership can destroy a good team of workers in any type of job, while good leadership can build and transform a bad team into a good team. Servant leadership is the key. More important than my opinion is this definition of servant leadership: "[It's] a leadership philosophy in which the main goal of the leader is to serve. This is different from traditional leadership where the leader's focus is the thriving of their company or organizations. A Servant Leader shares power, puts the needs of the employees first, and helps people develop and perform as highly as possible" (Greenleaf).

Subordinates should take on the concept of followership; they should be someone who is happy and willing to follow, someone that does not necessarily have the desire to be the leader, but is a team player and could take the leadership role if needed.

For example, in the army, a Sergeant has a Staff Sergeant above them and so on. Every rank or position will still have someone positioned above it. Even the President of the United States has the Congress who basically need to approve his/her wishes. Followership represents that person that is not only a subordinate but is completely aware of his/her role.

A good follower is willing to bring the team up and work together to complete any given task. Followership is proactive instead of reactive, and he/she should prepare ahead of the given task and should be efficient at their duties.

The following scenario is an example of good followership. PFC Doe looks at the time and notices that it's 1400 hours. He knows the last formation is at 1600 hours, so he starts cleaning before someone tells him to do that task. He is being proactive and a good team player.

As you can probably tell from the spelling of the word itself, followership means someone is meant to follow; that person is willing to accomplish the department goals and represent an important role for the leaders by motivating others, while also making the mission easier and effective for the leaders. Leaders lead the way by bringing up the team as well, and holding them at a higher standard.

A true leader takes care of their subordinates and coaches them to become better. A true leader identifies the skills on their team and focuses on their strengths. The leader's job is to lead from the front while the follower completes the mission, treats the subordinates well, motivates the team, and make the leader look great. When done well, it is a win/win situation.

Leadership	Followership
Elevates the team	Implied Tasks
Creates more leaders	Motivates the team
Leads by example	Elevates morale

In the graphic above, you will to see that followership falls into an effective follower (someone that reply with a yes, is a critical thinker and implied tasks are not an issue). Now you have a clear picture of servant leadership and followership. I compared them and gave examples on how they need each other. In all our ranks, we find good and bad leaders just like in every position.

We have good and bad politicians, pastors, teachers, soldiers, police, etc. We should maintain our focus on how to lift the good ones and create good leaders from those that are in the category of followership.

By putting our focus on those who deserve our time, whether is to work for them or to lead them, we will improve the organization's readiness, which will help it become more effective when is time to conduct a mission.

II. Critical Thinking & Problem-Solving Skills

Critical thinking and problem-solving skills are important and can affect us on a daily basis. Understanding that is the first step to become better. A while ago, I read a book called *The Four Agreements* by Don Miguel Ruiz. The following is an excerpt from that book:

Be Impeccable with Your Word

Speak with integrity. Say only what you mean. Avoid using the word to speak against yourself or to gossip about others. Use the power of your word in the direction of truth and love.

Be impeccable with yourself and that will reflect in your life and your relationships with others.

This agreement can help change thousands of other agreements, especially ones that create fear instead of love.

Don't Take Anything Personally

Nothing others do is because of you.

What others say and do is a projection of their own dream.

We take things personally when we agree with what others have said.

When we do not agree, the things that others say cannot affect us emotionally.

When we do not care about what others think about us, their words or behavior cannot affect us.

When someone yells at you, gossips about you, harms you or yours, it still is not about you!

Their actions and words are based on what they believe in their personal dream.

Don't Make Assumptions

Find the courage to ask questions and to express what you really want.

Communicate with others as clearly as you can to avoid misunderstandings, sadness, and drama.

With just this one agreement, you can completely transform your life.

When we make assumptions, it is because we believe we know what others are thinking and feeling.

We believe we know their point of view, their dream.

We forget that our beliefs are just our point of view based on our belief system and our own personal experiences that have nothing to do with what others think and feel.

We make the assumption that everybody judges us, abuses us, victimizes us, and blames us the way we do ourselves.

As a result we reject ourselves before others have the chance to reject us.

When we think this way, it becomes difficult to be ourselves in the world.

Take action and be clear to others about what you want or do not want; do not gossip and make assumptions about things others tell you.

Respect other points of view and avoid arguing just to be right.

Respect yourself and be honest with yourself.

Stop expecting the people around you to know what is in your head.

Always Do Your Best

Your best changes from moment to moment;

Your best is different when you are healthy as opposed to sick.

Simply do your best under any circumstance to avoid self-judgment, self-abuse, and regret.

Doing your best means enjoying the action without expecting a reward.

The pleasure comes from doing what you like in life and having fun, not from the reward or compensation.

Enjoy the path travelled and the destination will take care of itself. (Ruiz, 1997)

I always try to apply myself by those standards to become a better person; I think if everyone erases their bad experiences that formed their bad mentality and allow themselves to grow, this world would be better.

During an army leadership school session, we conducted a group activity where we had to mention different characteristics from a critical thinker and someone who is not a critical thinker. Some of the qualities the groups mentioned to describe a critical thinker were: prioritizes, get things done correctly, brings multiple ideas and options, thinks outside the box, analyzes everything, realizes the domino effect, is a leader, typically gets positive results, is open minded, adapts to changes, and is patient. Some of the non-critical thinker characteristics were that they jump to conclusions, they fail more often, they're lackadaisical, they make assumptions, they're nonchalant, they tend to be procrastinators, they never complete the mission or they complete it wrong, they're impatient, and followers. After the group activity, we continued to discuss the class and the importance of being a critical thinker.

One of the key points we talked about was basically having common sense, which included doing those implied tasks without someone telling you, like I mentioned before in the previous chapter.

In my opinion, high school students today should take a class called "Common Sense 101". It might sound silly, but after facing different situations in my life, I've concluded that common sense isn't common.

Here are some examples on how we can assist others to become a critical thinker:

- letting them handle small tasks

- giving them the opportunity to make small decisions
- giving them more time to accomplish a task and slowly shortened that time until they are proficient at that specific task

We are all different, and we come from different backgrounds/childhoods. That can affect anyone on how they are performing.

We have the authority and responsibility to make the change we want in our society. It's our time to start, and the change starts with you. I want to remind you that we are all natural leaders, it's just that sometimes we have been affected by our surroundings and the way our parents raised us, and that could either bring the best out of us or suppress our natural leadership skills.

Know that we can shine in our darkest moments, and we can lead by example knowing that we can always improve and develop leadership skills by using critical thinking. Think outside the box and make the difference.

III. Leader V. Boss

There is a big difference between a leader and a boss. A boss instructs you and tells you what to do; a leader makes you feel like you want to do it. A leader leads from the front and see the subordinates like a family or a team. He would never request you to do something that he is not willing to do himself. I have seen friends and jobs where the boss destroys a great team. I have also seen a leader bringing up a "bad" team, turning them into a great team.

Elite Daily post an article written by Abdullayeva mentioning 7 important key points and I will explain them based on my experience and courses taken.

1. Leaders lead rather than rule
   No one wants a grumpy boss that tells you what to do and micromanage every task. A true leader will not only tell you but show you what to do, is not afraid of getting dirty leading by example.

2. Leaders listen and speak rather than command.
   A Command Sergeant Major in my Brigade said: "The day I need to raise my voice I'm no longer a Command Sergeant Major" – Anonymous

   With that he sent a clear message that giving commands loud is not a true representation of authority, with that being said there is a time and place for everything i.e. If someone is doing something unsafe it is necessary to intervene and probably will require a loud voice, but when referring to the overall leadership a true leader should be a mentor more than a ruler and a speaker more than someone that yells to feel that he is bigger than their subordinates. A true leader understands the definition of a team player and that his/her role is just lead that team.

3. Leaders motivate rather than terrify.
   Just like mentioned above, a true leader will inspire you, will motivate you to become better not only for the mission or task to be accomplished but to become a better version of you. A true leader will create more leaders, sharing their knowledge.

4. Leaders teach and learn rather than expect and ignore.
    A leader will teach and become a mentor, not only
    demanding the standard but showing you the standard
    instead of just making a request and expect you will
    perform as he expected.

5. Leaders take part rather than stay aside.
    Like I mentioned in point #1, Leaders take part of
    the mission/task and not only supervise but show
    how is supposed to be done not in a micromanaging
    perspective but in the "standard" perspective. To
    include listen to his/her subordinates' ideas and
    showing them respect.

6. Leaders reprimand rather than scold or shout.
    Like I mentioned in point 2 with the Command
    Sergeant Major example, during my Military time
    I have learned that you get better results by praising
    in public and reprimand in private. That method is
    also used in the parent/son relationship and is very
    effective.

7. Leaders establish equal relationships.
    Preference is something that create a bad atmosphere
    at work. Equal relationships means that I should treat
    everyone the same way and neutral, regardless of their
    position. My mom raised me by teaching me that I
    should treat everyone with the same respect regardless
    of their position.

CHAPTER 4

THE POWER
OF WORDS

"²⁹ Do not let any unwholesome talk come out
of your mouths, but only what is helpful for
building others up according to their needs,
that it may benefit those who listen."

Ephesians 4:29 (NIV)

Our words can build or destroy someone. Everything we know was developed by someone's words. If you believe in a higher power, you most likely believe that spoken words created the universe and this planet, along with every life-form on it. Words spoken by Adolf Hitler killed millions during his reign, words made Egyptians built the pyramids, and words created and destroyed empires. Words can lift someone from depression and words can also take someone down by mentally draining their energy.

Something I continue to develop every day is utilizing the power of words. In the military and Law enforcement field words can be the difference between life or death. They can be the difference between escalating or deescalating a situation.

They can bring a suspect down without a use of force and they can save a suicidal person by preventing him from jumping off a bridge.

With words, sorcerers and witches have casted spells. With words, Moses opened the Red Sea. With words, Moses turned his staff into a snake, with the power of God. With words, Pharaoh's magicians turned their staffs into snakes as well.

With words, a president can unify or divide a country. With words, the media controls society as they please, and most of the people are too busy to do research about the information presented and they become followers of false information.

We need to be aware of the pros and cons of the words. If used wisely, they can change your life and subsequently, the world. I'm a dad of a 9 year old boy, and I always do my best to encourage him to do better, to shine, and to do the right thing even when no one is watching. The words I speak to him will become the assets of his future that he will always remember. As a parent, my words have a greater impact when they are backed up by my actions. No matter where you go, make sure you speak life. Be an uplifting person. Be someone others look up to for advice and as a role model.

Now that I mentioned the importance of words, it's our job to prevent others' words from affecting us, and to use active listening skills from our mentors.

Interpersonal communication skills are everything in our lives. I can be smart, but by not having those skills, I might get a to certain point, but I won't be able to reach my full potential until I allow myself to learn and develop interpersonal communication skills.

There are different communications styles: Direct, Indirect, Low Context, High Context, Task, Relationship, Formal, and Informal. Understand that we always have several options when sending and receiving messages. We need to be selective and the situation will dictate what is the appropriate method.

Those communication skills will follow you everywhere you go and will make an impact on everyone you get in contact with. Some examples are:

"Could you please close the door?"
or you could say,
"Close the damn door."

Which one do you think will have a better response?
Get that door opened or closed?

I always believe that is not what I say but how I say it. And that's the key behind interpersonal communications skills.

I personally like to shape myself to my audience. For example, If I'm talking to a kid or my son, I like to kneel to their height. That will put me at his/her level, allowing me to get my point across with better results. If I'm talking to an audience that is very professional (doctors, professors, etc.), I will talk more directly; I will use more complicated words to prepare myself before that conversation. As a Sheriff's Corporal in the civilian law enforcement, I use these skills on a daily basis. It allows me to engage and even deescalate a potentially dangerous situation.

The most important thing for me is leaving assumptions at home and never taking a situation personally. That way, we become active listeners.

It's worth it to mention that I've lived 23+ years in Puerto Rico, with Spanish being my primary language and the only English reading skills are the ones that I learned over my grade school years. I never let this language barrier stop my dreams though. I still have a nice and strong Hispanic accent that I proudly pronounce, but my mentality is to improve in everything I do. My Grandfather died more than 15 years ago, and something I still carry from him was his advice. I remember my Grandpa saying, "It doesn't matter who you want to be or what you want to do, whatever you do, do your best. I don't care if is performing janitor duties, doing dishes, being a dad, cutting grass, or being a politician, always do your best."

The language and my Grandpa's advice are part of my active listening skills and I still carry them with me every day.

Here is another example of active listening:

I was working for the Brevard County Sherriff's Office. (mention you were working in the jail?) A suspect was arrested for DUI, and after arriving at the jail, the suspect started to yell obscenities at the booking deputies and the situation was getting out of control because of passive resistance and because the booking deputies were not following the simple instructions to conduct the search of the suspect prior to removing his handcuffs. While trying to deal with the arrestee,

I noticed a military tattoo on his arm. I immediately changed the approach and asked him, "Are you prior service?" He replied, "Yes, I served in the Army."

I utilized that common ground we had by identifying myself as a soldier with my MOS and unit. It seemed to be like magic, because the suspect stated: "I don't want anyone else to deal with me but you." I was able to get the suspect through the entire booking process, which includes fingerprints, pictures, and the arrest form with no further incidents.

Everyone in the booking room was surprised about how the suspect changed his entire behavior by only finding someone who could relate with him.

> *"Show that you can talk to anyone, demonstrate your ability to convey information usefully, focus on team success, illustrate your capacity to remain calm under pressure, exhibit how you fit into company culture."* (Kea)

In summary, Kea mentioned that we need to adapt to our environment, and communicate well with others to make sure that our point gets across without any misunderstandings. Understand the power of teamwork, be levelheaded, and remain calm and professional, even when you find yourself in stressful situations.

Last but not least, we need to be able to fit in the culture of our jobs. That way, we remain flexible and allow ourselves to grow; someone told me a while ago that to learn new things, we need to empty any previous knowledge and allow us to learn new things; that's the key to success.

So, to be able to learn new things, remember that you can express anything, but you need to also be an active listener. That will help with jobs, relationships, and will make you a great leader. Be the change this world needs. To become an active listener, look at the eyes of the person you're speaking with, ask questions, and show interest and respect for them.

CHAPTER 5

A DIFFERENT PERSPECTIVE

¹²There is a way that appears to be right,
but in the end, it leads to death.

Proverbs 14:12

As of now, the Bible is still the one of the most famous books in the world. And regardless of your religious beliefs, the Bible contains great values and can be a good guide on how to live your life. It contains moral standards and great stories that provide a different perspective in our busy modern lives. In the next few pages, you will find some Bible verses that show how important and powerful our words are.

"Likewise, the tongue is a small part of the body, but it makes great boasts. Consider what a great forest is set on fire by a small spark. ⁶The tongue also is a fire, a world of evil among the parts of the body. It corrupts the whole body, sets the whole course of one's life on fire, and is itself set on fire by hell. ⁷All kinds of animals, birds, reptiles and sea creatures are being tamed and have been tamed by mankind, ⁸but no human being can tame the tongue. It is a restless evil, full of deadly poison." **James 3:5-8 NIV**

The tongue is extremely powerful; it can command an army, build a person up or destroy them, tame animals, govern a country, and even kill or save someone.

Knowing this, we have two duties in life:

#1 Tame your tongue. If what you are about to say is not going to contribute positively to something or provide a solution, build someone up, or is not positive in general, refrain from saying it.

#2 Knowing this, when someone verbally attacks you or attempts to put you down, be wise. Sometimes remaining in silence is the best defense you could ever have.

"Death and life are in the power of the tongue, and those who love it will eat its fruits." -**Proverbs 18:21 KJV**

The wise king Solomon wrote the book of Proverbs; as mentioned above, the power of death and life are in the tongue. Those who fall for it can be consumed.

"I tell you, on the day of judgment people will give account for every careless word they speak, for by your words you will be justified, and by your words you will be condemned." -**Matthew 12:36-37 KJV**

In this verse, it's mentioned how you can be justified or condemned by your words. It's imperative that we understand than even though the verse is talking about the final day of judgement for all, it's still an accurate representation of our words on a daily basis. I have seen people getting destroyed because they used the wrong words. I have seen the smartest person losing everything and the average person gaining the world because they understood the importance of the words they chose to use.

"Either make the tree good and its fruit good, or make the tree bad and its fruit bad, for the tree is known by its fruit. You brood of vipers! How can you speak good, when you are evil? For out of the abundance of the heart the mouth speaks. The good person out of his good treasure brings forth good, and the evil person out of his evil treasure brings forth evil." -**Matthew 12:33-35 NIV**

Words are a reflection of yourself. You can identify where someone's heart is just by listening to them speak. Words are sometimes supported by actions, but actions don't need words. Actions speak a lot louder than anything you could say. Apply that concept to customers, family, and intimate relations. That will show them that you are genuine. Always let your actions show the best representation of you, but don't forget that words will also speak to the intentions of your heart.

> "Let no corrupting talk come out of your mouths, but only such as is good for building up, as fits the occasion, that it may give grace to those who hear." -**Ephesians 4:29 ESV**

Stay positive, and change the atmosphere for the better wherever you go. You will notice that people will look up to you. Be that person!

> "Whoever guards his mouth preserves his life; he who opens wide his lips comes to ruin."- **Proverbs 13:3 NIV**

Basically, this verse establishes that sometimes it's better to stay quiet. How many times do we say hurtful things during a moment of anger? When we do that, typically someone gets hurt, and we end up regretting it, but the words you spoke cannot ever be taken back. So be careful.

> "There is one whose rash words are like sword thrusts, but the tongue of the wise brings healing." - **Proverbs 12:18 NRS**

This verse is an amazing one. An experiment was conducted by the television show, "MythBusters" called

"Talking to Plants" and it showed how words have control over nature, and therefore, our bodies.

Here were the results:

"To give the myth a fighting chance of flourishing, the team charted the plants' growth over 60 days. Afterward, the MythBusters determined the winning greenhouse by comparing plant masses from the three groups. To their surprise, the silent greenhouse performed poorest, producing lower biomass and smaller pea pods than the other two. Although there was no difference in plant quality between the nice greenhouse and the mean greenhouse, the soundtracks seemed to produce a positive effect in both." (Hemera/Thinkstock, n.d.)

C H A P T E R **6**

STARTING FROM ZERO

"The beginning is always NOW." (Benneth, n.d.)

-Roy T. Bennett

Since I was a kid, I worked in car detailing, helping someone or even volunteering for community service, etc. I was 15 years old when I started working in the production of music and art design on the beautiful island of Puerto Rico.

I remember when I told my dad that I was choosing this path, but making music didn't sound like a "career" to him, so he didn't support me until almost 2 years later when he saw results from my efforts. I was young and full of energy, so for almost 5 years, I dedicated my life to the production of music and art designs. That's also when I found out that the ones who should've been supportive of my dreams became skeptical. The friends that wanted work done were the first ones asking for a discount, and surprisingly, the strangers were the ones that actually supported my business.

It was hard but motivational, and I never let anyone or anything to discourage my dreams.

During that time, I got married, and 2 years later, I had my son, who became my everything and my inspiration to grow and do better. I didn't understand what love was until I became a father. In 2010, we moved to Connecticut to work on some music projects and we ended up starting from zero (for the second time). At the time, Connecticut was having the worst cold weather in the last 10 years, or at least that's what friends told me, and with me being from Puerto Rico, which has tropical weather all year round, it was really hard to get used to the cold and learn how to drive in the snow and ice. I would have to write a whole other book on how I feel about driving in the snow!

After several months, it was 2011, and we had finished the production and traveled back to Puerto Rico.

As I grew up, I had always dreamed about being in the military, or working in the law enforcement field. I was always involved in the leadership/staff at my church, and also politics on the Island (yes, you can do both). Following my childhood passion in 2012, I joined the army and became a military police officer, and then I started college and worked hard to be a good provider. A year later, we moved to Florida, and for the third time, we started from zero.

I first traveled for the interview and got the job. Now this was the type of situation where your actions need to be lined up with your faith and words. After I got accepted for the job, I traveled back to Puerto Rico, sold our belongings, and a week later, I got an apartment lease in Florida, got a car, and got everything ready for the new job. I remember that was around December 11th, 2013. Three weeks passed, and I still didn't have the job. At that point, my faith was getting to the limit and praying didn't seem like it was enough. It wasn't until mid-January 2014 that I finally started working for them.

It was a very scary situation but I want to use this example because if your faith or words are empty, and not backed up by your actions, they're nothing. I gave my best at the time, but was so looking forward to joining a law enforcement agency. I achieved my goal, but it felt like a long road to get there. Then, unfortunately, after several years in the military, I became part of the statistics for the military divorce rate. After 10 years of marriage, I ended up getting divorced. Even at my darkest moment, though, I was able to shine because my vision never changed. When you have a clear vision, you might still need to adjust the mission sometimes, but how you're going to execute the plan should remain the same.

Thankfully, my ex-wife and I maintain good communication, and our main goal is the well-being of our son. Everything we do will have consequences, for good or bad, just like a habit can be either good or bad. The ups and down in life are what keep us alive, and the experiences we have will make us stronger, so when you fall, GET BACK UP! Learn and move on.

The following are Bible verses that helped me in my journey to become stronger and focused during times of need or the times that I wanted to stop every time I started from zero.

> [11] But the LORD is with me as a terrible one: therefore, my persecutors shall stumble, and they shall not prevail: they shall be greatly ashamed; for they shall not prosper: their everlasting confusion shall never be forgotten. **-Jeremiah 20:11 (KJV)**
>
> [11]For I know the plans I have for you," declares the LORD, "plans to prosper you and not to harm you, plans to give you hope and a future. **-Jeremiah 29:11 NIV**
>
> [28]And we know that in all things God works for the good of those who love him, who have been called according to his purpose. **-Romans 8:28 KJV**

Those bible verses were my inspiration during the hard times I've been through. I've learned that faith is real and that nothing can stop me if my Lord is by my side.

CHAPTER 7

ONCE AGAIN

⁵ He who was seated on the throne said,
"I am making everything new!"

Then he said, "Write this down, for these
words are trustworthy and true."

Revelation 21:5 (NIV)

I believe that situations do not have to dictate your reaction, mood, or behavior. We have control over our body and mind. If we allow external factors to alter our life, then we are being manipulated by everything that surrounds us. Self-control and discipline are some of the traits that you will find in a successful person. During that period of time between 2016 and 2017, my military unit was mobilized to Central America. With the leadership courses, schools, training, and experiences, I became a different person. I was no longer affected by outside factors, I learned a couple of life lessons, and I moved on.

I remember I was driving with my son once and got a flat tire; I was in a rush because I was dealing with a lot of situations at once. Instead of becoming angry or upset, I grounded myself and said to my son, "Son, today is a good day to learn something new. I will teach you how to change a tire." Those words made a difference, and the way I reacted gave him peace after the incident. I'm far from perfect, but sharing these personal experiences will allow me to honestly share my life and perhaps give you a different perspective for your own life.

Since I changed my mentality and applied the concepts explained in the first few chapters about leadership, listening skills, how the brain works, and the power of words, I was recipient of several awards from serving in the Military and working for the Brevard County Sheriff's Office. Some of the awards I received are: The Melbourne Regional Chamber Valor Award in 2018, the Brevard County Sheriff's Office Merit Award in 2017, the Army Commendation Medal in 2016, several Army Achievement medals, etc.

I've also had the privilege to work in different positions of leadership throughout my career.

We have the power to change the world, and to become an agent of change to those surrounding us.

How many times have you inspired others?
How many times have you provided advice?

Regardless of your situation and/or position you have the responsibility to not only shine in what you do, but to also enlighten others. Be that support system for someone, and if knowledge is the issue then get the knowledge; if education is the missing item, then get that education you need.

Procrastination is leaving for tomorrow what you can get done today. Don't ever procrastinate. Be that person that gets stuff done, and that will make you an asset wherever you work or study. If I had waited for "the right time" to accomplish everything I ever wanted to do, I would have never joined the military, had a kid, got my college courses done, joined the Sheriff Department, etc. There is no such thing as the right time. The right time is now! Today! Get out of your comfort zone and go get it. The universe is waiting for you to go after what belongs to you. As of February 2019, I created a Tactical Training company, Early and Often Tactical (E&O Tactical LLC), assembled an amazing team and opened the doors of a nice location to offer services to Security companies, individuals and the community. The time is now.

Keep a positive attitude and you will never regret anything. Success is the line between opportunity and preparation. Create the opportunity while you prepare yourself; this will be a life changer for you and those around you.

SUMMARY

I have no words to express my gratitude, for this is my first publication and I'm so grateful for your support. The basic guidelines given in this book are just some building blocks and the foundation of a successful life. Your attitude, your words, and perspective will boost and enhance your life in every aspect. Understand that everyone is on a different level in life, so never compare yourself with someone else's success. You should be your own competition, compare yourself with the old you from yesterday: what are you doing today better than yesterday? Keep in mind that it doesn't have to take 21 days for you to form or break a habit. You could have the discipline to do either one in just a few days! For the most part, though, consistency is the key for you to become a successful person.

Remember that to be a good leader you need to be a good student, or follower, first. Also, surround yourself with people that lift you up and help you to become better. Stay away from dream destroyers that can only see the negative side in everything, and a problem for every solution.

Be the kind of leader that you would follow, and never ask someone to do something that you wouldn't do. Avoid repeating the mistakes you see in other leaders.

Become a master with your words, learn to stay quiet, or your words won't be as beneficial to others. Understand the law of attraction, and the things you proclaim will have an effect in this universe. Set goals, conquer them, you have the power in your hands. Become everything you want to be.

-John

REFERENCES

Abdullayeva, L. (2014, April 18). *Elite Daily*. Retrieved from https://www.elitedaily.com/money/entrepreneurship/ things-distinguishes-leader-boss

ARMY. (2018). Critical Thinking and Problem-Solving skills. RTI.

Benneth, R. T. (n.d.).

Einstein, A. (n.d.). 1879-1955.

Franklin, B. (n.d.). proverb.

Greenleaf, R. (n.d.). *Wikipedia*. Retrieved from https:// en.wikipedia.org/wiki/Servant_leadership

Hemera/Thinkstock, M. /. (n.d.). *Discovery.com*. Retrieved from http://www.discovery.com/tv-shows/mythbusters/ mythbusters-database/talking-to-plants/

Hess, A. (2017, AUG). *CNBC*. Retrieved from https://www. cnbc.com/2017/08/25/heres-why-lottery-winners-go-broke.html

Kea, K. (n.d.). Retrieved from ziprecuiter.com: https:// www.ziprecruiter.com/blog/how-developing-your-interpersonal-skills-will-help-you-get-ahead/

Kelly, M. (2016, Sept). *Renewing gall things*. Retrieved from https://renewingallthings.com/spiritual-health/ habits-science-change-class/

Kid Sense. (n.d.). Retrieved from Child Development: https://childdevelopment.com.au/areas-of-concern/ gross-motor-skills/gross-motor-skills/

Lally, P. (2009, July 16). *How are habits formed: Modelling habit formation in the real world.* Retrieved from https:// onlinelibrary.wiley.com/doi/full/10.1002/ejsp.674

Ruiz, M. (1997). *The Four Agreements.* Retrieved from https:// en.wikipedia.org/wiki/Don_Miguel_Ruiz

Unknown. (n.d.). Common Proverb. unknown.

Wikipedia. (n.d.). Retrieved from https://en.wikipedia.org/ wiki/Fine_motor_skill

Woodward, O. (n.d.).

Printed in the United States
By Bookmasters